NOT A SILENT NIGHT

MARY LOOKS BACK TO BETHLEHEM

Not a Silent Night
Mary Looks Back to Bethlehem

Not a Silent Night
978-1-5018-7957-9 *Book*
978-1-63088-295-2 *Large Print*
978-1-5018-7957-9 *eBook*

Not a Silent Night: DVD
978-1-4267-7185-9

Not a Silent Night: Leader Guide
978-1-63088-035-4
978-1-5018-1572-0 *eBook*

Not a Silent Night: Youth Study Book
978-1-5018-1569-0
978-1-5018-1570-6 *eBook*

Also by Adam Hamilton

24 Hours That Changed the World

Christianity's Family Tree

Confronting the Controversies

Creed

Enough

Faithful

Final Words from the Cross

Forgiveness

Half Truths

John

Leading Beyond the Walls

Love to Stay

Making Sense of the Bible

Moses

Not a Silent Night

Revival

Seeing Gray in a World of Black and White

Selling Swimsuits in the Arctic

Speaking Well

The Call

The Journey

The Way

Unafraid

Unleashing the Word

When Christians Get It Wrong

Why?

For more information, visit www.AdamHamilton.org.

ADAM HAMILTON

NOT A
SILENT NIGHT

MARY LOOKS BACK TO BETHLEHEM

Abingdon Press / Nashville

NOT A SILENT NIGHT:
MARY LOOKS BACK TO BETHLEHEM

**Library of Congress Cataloging in Publication data is on file under
hardcover edition.**

ISBN 978-1-5018-7957-9 (first paperback edition)
First hardcover edition published in 2014 as ISBN 978-1-426-77184-2.

18 19 20 21 22 23 24 25 26 27 — 10 9 8 7 6 5 4 3 2 1
MANUFACTURED IN THE UNITED STATES OF AMERICA

To my granddaughter,
Stella Louise Hamilton Slate,
who makes me smile every time I see her

CONTENTS

INTRODUCTION

THE STORY
THROUGH MARY'S EYES

Silent night, holy night,
all is calm, all is bright
round yon virgin mother and child.
Holy infant, so tender and mild,
sleep in heavenly peace,
sleep in heavenly peace.[1]

Silent Night. From the carols we sing to the art on
our Christmas cards, we are surrounded by images
of the serene young Mary in clean, beautiful robes,

holding the calm baby. Who is she? Was that what that night was really like? How did this young mother remember it in the years to follow?

We have a picture of what that first Christmas must have been like for the young mother: perfect, starlit, holy. The reality, however, was not unlike our own lives. There was joy, but it was mixed with pain and sorrow, uncertainty and adversity. This was true throughout her life, with blessings and pain intermingled.

This year we'll be preparing our hearts for Christmas by looking at Jesus' life through Mary's eyes. In focusing on Mary, we're going to do something a bit unusual. We'll tell her story by starting not at the beginning but at the end. In the first chapter we'll start with Mary's death and the last years of her life. Then in each succeeding chapter we'll work our way backward, from the Crucifixion and Jesus' ministry, to his discovery in the Temple as a twelve-year-old boy, to the announcement of the Savior to come, until finally we will end on Christmas Day with the birth of Jesus. In each chapter we'll consider the meaning of the birth of Jesus by looking at the significance of his life, death, and resurrection.

I invite you to travel with me and experience the story of a not-so-silent night, of a young mother unexpectedly chosen by God to bring the Christ Child into the world. Along the way, we will discover the gifts she received at each stage of his life, and we will receive them too: the hope of resurrection found in the garden, the salvation gift of the cross, a new way to live that Jesus taught in his ministry, and the ever-present gift of God's grace.

As Mary learned, God doesn't promise a perfect, peaceful life or a silent, holy night. She was blessed, God-favored, and grace-filled, yet her troubles did not end. That's how life was for Mary, and that's how life is for us. Life doesn't go according to our plans. Sometimes it's hard and painful and scary. Yet, in the messiness of life, God is at work, bringing blessing out of pain. That's the message of Christmas.

1.

BEGINNING
WITH THE END

"You will receive power when the Holy Spirit has come upon you; and you will be my witnesses in Jerusalem, in all Judea and Samaria, and to the ends of the earth." When he [Jesus] had said this, as they were watching, he was lifted up, and a cloud took him out of their sight. While he was going and they were gazing up toward heaven, suddenly two men in white robes stood by them. They said, "Men of Galilee, why do you stand looking up toward heaven? This Jesus, who has been taken up from you into heaven, will come in the same way as you saw him go into heaven."

Then they returned to Jerusalem from the mount called Olivet, which is near Jerusalem, a sabbath day's journey away. When they had entered the city, they went to the room upstairs where they were staying, Peter, and John, and James, and Andrew, Philip and Thomas, Bartholomew and Matthew, James son of Alphaeus, and Simon the Zealot, and Judas son of James. All these were constantly devoting themselves to prayer, together with certain women, including Mary the mother of Jesus, as well as his brothers. (Acts 1:8-14)

1.

BEGINNING WITH THE END

Christmas comes on December 25, but for many Americans it starts before that: on Black Friday, the day after Thanksgiving. The newspaper announces glad tidings of great joy with five pounds of advertisements. Big-screen TVs for several hundred dollars—can you believe it? Blu-ray players for next to nothing. The entire stock of men's clothing at 50 percent off. Unbelievable deals. And the stores open their doors at three, four, five o'clock in the morning. I mean, that's good news!

Several years ago the good news turned to tragedy for a Walmart employee on Long Island, New York.[2] You may remember the story. Jdimytai Damour was a part-time seasonal worker at Walmart who had just started working there. His job was to stock the shelves in the morning. He arrived early that Friday and was assigned to stand by the door at 4:55 a.m. There were two thousand people standing outside in the cold, eager to get a great buy on a TV or a jacket or some other sale item.

The door looked like it was going to open, then it closed again. The people were frustrated and agitated. They were cold and ready to go inside. Some of them pounded on the glass doors. Others pushed on the doors, and as they did they noticed there was some give in them. The crowd surged forward. They pressed into the glass, the glass shattered, and the frame landed on top of

Jdimytai Damour. The people rushed in to get their bargains, like a herd of cattle. They saw Jdimytai lying there. Some stepped over him, and some stepped on him. Even knowing he was hurt, people went on with their shopping, buying Christmas presents, making sure they got what they had waited for.

Before the morning was over, in spite of attempts to administer CPR, Jdimytai Damour was pronounced dead. It's a story of Christmas run amok, and it's symbolic of something bigger—a kind of amnesia, illustrating how ordinary people forget the real meaning of Christmas.

> Advent is a time when we prepare ourselves spiritually to celebrate the birth of the Savior.

Advent is the church's response to this amnesia. Advent is a four-week period when Christians pause and say, "Let's remember what this is all about.

Let's remember who the child is, born in Bethlehem two thousand years ago. Let's remember the hope and promise that come from him. Let's remember who he called us to be and what he called us to do. Let's remember the mission he gave us as we seek to live as Christ-followers." Advent is a time when we prepare ourselves spiritually to celebrate the birth of the Savior. The word *advent* comes from a Latin word that means "coming." During that four-week period we not only prepare to commemorate Christ's first advent, his birth in Bethlehem; we also prepare for the day when Christ will return, in glory, to usher in a new heaven and earth.

It is customary during Advent for churches to focus on the prophets, or John the Baptist, or the stories surrounding Jesus' birth. In this book we'll take a different approach. We'll explore Advent and the meaning of Christmas by focusing on Mary's perspective of her son. No one was closer to Jesus than Mary. No one shaped his life more than she did. No one knew him better, nor loved him more. And no other human being paid a greater price than she did for his birth, life, and death. Mary's own life was not blissful, peaceful, and blessed. It was challenging, painful, and at times filled with sorrow. Yet despite this, Mary "magnifies the Lord" and "rejoices in God," as she tells us in her joyful song, the Magnificat (Luke 1:46-55).

But it is not just exploring the meaning of Christ's birth through the eyes of Mary that makes this little book unique. Others have done the same, looking at the events in Mary's life leading up to the birth of Jesus. Rather, in this book we'll start not before the birth of Jesus but decades after. We'll begin at the end of Mary's life, years after Jesus' death and resurrection. Each week we'll journey back in time to key events in the life of Jesus as seen through Mary's eyes, until finally we arrive at the night he was born.

There's only one verse that mentions Mary by name after the resurrection of Christ.

Mary's Final Years

Let's begin at the end of Mary's life, with what we know about Mary's final years and her death. It's a challenge to discuss Mary's last years, because there's not much known about them. Here the Bible is virtually silent. There's only one verse that mentions Mary by name after the resurrection of Christ. We're told in Acts 1:14 that, following Jesus' ascension and before the outpouring of the Spirit at Pentecost, the disciples and "certain women, including Mary the mother of Jesus, as well as his brothers" constantly devoted themselves to prayer.

With little information about the rest of Mary's life found in Scripture, our only sources of information are the traditions that developed in the church during the centuries following her death. Some details are undoubtedly legendary; others may point us toward facts. In Roman Catholic and Eastern Orthodox churches, these stories are an important part of the church's liturgical year, while Protestants are not likely to be as familiar with them.

Roman Catholic and Eastern Orthodox Christians commemorate Mary's death on August 15 each year. Roman Catholics celebrate this as the Feast of the Assumption and Orthodox Christians as the Feast of the Dormition. The two different names point to similar ideas held by Catholic and Orthodox Christians concerning what happened at Mary's death.

Roman Catholics believe that Mary was taken up bodily to heaven shortly after her burial (though some suggest she did not actually die, the consensus is that she died) as a special way in which Mary was honored by God as God had done with Enoch and Elijah in the Old Testament. Enoch and Elijah were righteous people who were "taken up" or assumed into heaven without experiencing death. In Genesis 5:24 we read, "Enoch walked with God; then he was no more, because God took him." In Second Kings we read that Elijah was taken up to heaven in a chariot of fire (2:11).

Orthodox Christians believe that Mary died—the euphemism they use is that she "fell asleep"—and on the third day after dying, her body was taken up to heaven. The Latin word for "sleep" is *dormitio*, thus the Feast of the Dormition recalls Mary's death and subsequent bodily assumption to heaven.

While we have no scriptural evidence for Mary's assumption, throughout most of church history starting at least in the fifth century, if not before, Christians believed Mary was taken up to heaven shortly after her death.

One version of the story tells that three days before her death, Mary was visited by the angel Gabriel, the same angel who came to her when she was a girl of thirteen or fourteen to announce that she would give birth to the Christ. At this second appearance Gabriel looked no older than before, but Mary would have been, by some accounts in the early church, around sixty (some accounts in the early church suggest fifty- nine years of age, and other accounts suggest she was sixty-four years old). Gabriel announced to Mary that in three days she would die, and, hearing this, Mary asked to see the apostles one last time. The apostles were scattered around the world preaching the gospel, but the story has it that the Holy Spirit supernaturally gathered all of them, including Paul, around Mary's bedside. Only Thomas was unable to be present.

Mary was then laid to rest in a tomb. Thomas arrived three days later, according to the story, and when he arrived he asked to see Mary's body. When the crypt was opened, the disciples found, much to their surprise, that Mary's body was gone and only her burial shroud remained!

In addition to the debate over how Mary died and whether she was taken to heaven before death, there is the debate over where Mary was buried. Many Christians believe that Mary died in Jerusalem and was buried in a cave adjacent to the Garden of Gethsemane on the Mount of Olives. You can visit this cave and see the supposed tomb of Mary.

Some Christians say that the place where Mary died was Ephesus in western Turkey. The Apostle John lived out his days there, and since Jesus had entrusted his mother to John it is thought that Mary lived out her days with John in Ephesus. If you visit Ephesus you'll be taken to a chapel called the House of the Virgin, near which some believe Mary was buried. Inside the chapel is an altar table dedicated to the memory of the Virgin Mary. It's a peaceful place, and outside there's a wall where you can put your prayer concerns.

Protestants are more cautious than Catholics and Orthodox Christians about traditions such as these, which are not rooted in Scripture. But whether you believe the stories or not, they focus our attention on one thing that Protestants, Catholics, and Orthodox agree upon: the resurrection of the dead. How Mary's death happened is not as important to me as the fact that as she approached death she undoubtedly believed that when she died, she would see her son once again.

> Among the greatest gifts God has given us at Christmas is the hope that "death has been swallowed up in victory" (1 Corinthians 15:54).

The Hope of Resurrection

At the Church of the Resurrection each year in December, we hold a special worship service for everyone who lost a loved one that year. We recognize that Christmas itself can intensify the feelings of loss and grief. At that service we remember that Christmas is inextricably linked to Easter. The child whose birth we celebrate would one day conquer death. Among the greatest gifts God has given us at Christmas is the hope that "death has been swallowed up in victory" (1 Corinthians 15:54). The infant Jesus would grow up to say, "I am the resurrection and the life. Those who believe in me, even though they die, will live, and everyone who lives and believes in me will never die" (John 11:25-26).

Pope John Paul II suggested that at Jesus' resurrection, before he appeared to Mary Magdalene or anyone else, he first appeared to his mother. The pope suggested that this was why, when Mary Magdalene first arrived at the tomb, Jesus was not there.[3] Of course, we cannot know whether the pope's supposition is true, but it seems to me Jesus would most certainly have appeared to his mother after his resurrection. The Scripture passage from Acts 1 mentioned previously seems to imply that Mary was present at the ascension of Jesus, and so, at the very least, she would have seen him then.

Mary witnessed the terrible and tragic death of her son. Then she had the joy of seeing Christ resurrected from the dead. But then, forty days later, she witnessed him leaving once more in the Ascension. If Mary died around age sixty, as one tradition suggests, it meant that she lived roughly fifteen years after Jesus' death on the cross, his resurrection, and his ascension to heaven.

I have been with many parents who have lost children. They have told me that the pain changes over time but the sense of loss is carried with them the rest of their lives. They survive. Over time they discover joy again. But there is always that sense of loss that parents feel for their children.

One woman whose son died in a tragic accident told me that she feels a connection to Mary, who also experienced the death of her son:

> When you lose a child, you lose part of yourself as a woman. He was inside you. He was your flesh and blood. I just feel her pain, watching what he went through. It is

absolutely catastrophic devastation at first. You eventually come to peace with it. You know he's in a better place. You know you're going to see him again. You view heaven in totally different ways than other people do. You deal with grief in different ways. Mine was in coming closer to the Lord.

> The Resurrection changed how Mary experienced her grief: it gave her hope.

The appearance of Jesus to Mary after his death would have changed everything for her. She still would have carried the grief of his suffering with her. She would have carried the sense of separation and loss that any of us would feel after the death of someone so close to us. But the Resurrection, we can be sure, changed how Mary experienced her grief: it gave her hope.

The Apostle Paul wrote the following words to the church at Thessalonica after several key members of

the church, beloved family of people who were part
of the congregation, had died:

> We do not want you to be uninformed,
> brothers and sisters, about those who have
> died, so that you may not grieve as others do
> who have no hope. For since we believe that
> Jesus died and rose again, even so, through
> Jesus, God will bring with him those who
> have died. . . . For the Lord himself, with a
> cry of command, with the archangel's call
> and with the sound of God's trumpet, will
> descend from heaven, and the dead in Christ
> will rise first. Then we who are alive, who are
> left, will be caught up in the clouds together
> with them to meet the Lord in the air; and so
> we will be with the Lord forever. Therefore
> encourage one another with these words.
> (1 Thessalonians 4:13-14, 16-18)

Paul calls us to encourage one another with the
hope that this life is not all there is. Encourage one
another with the fact that you'll see your loved ones
again. Encourage one another with the prospect that
the world will not always be as it is now. This is part

of the promise and hope of Christmas—that the One who was born in Bethlehem will set all things right one day.

Paul devotes the entire fifteenth chapter of First Corinthians to this view of the Resurrection. He concludes with these powerful words: "When this perishable body puts on imperishability, and this mortal body puts on immortality, then the saying that is written will be fulfilled: 'Death has been swallowed up in victory'" (1 Corinthians 15:54).

My grandfather died over twenty years ago on his ninetieth birthday. In the morning we had taken balloons to him for his birthday. In the evening the nurses called and said, "Your grandfather is not going to make it through the night." So I went to sit with him as he was dying. I took water from the tap and sprinkled it on his head, reminding him that in his baptism, which had occurred almost ninety years before, God had claimed him and had promised to wash him clean and give him life. My grandfather began to breathe in a more labored way, and I whispered in his ear as I held his hand, "Grandpa, it's okay. It's okay. You don't have to fight. You can just let go. Just trust God. He's got you in his hands. Let go, Grandpa. It's all right." Then I said this: "Grandpa, I will see you again someday. I will see you again." I can imagine Jesus saying this to Mary the last time he spoke to her. I imagine he would have looked at her and said, "Mother, I *will* see you again someday."

This is the hope we find in Christmas. Our first Christmas after the death of a loved one may be particularly hard. But such grief may be borne when we remember that the Christ whose birth we celebrate conquered the grave and gives us hope we will see our loved ones again.

Mary's Mission and Ours

There is one final question I invite you to consider in this chapter. What do you think Mary was doing from the time Jesus ascended to heaven until her own death?

Mary seems to have been present at Jesus' ascension. It was there that he said to his disciples, "Go therefore and make disciples of all nations, baptizing them in the name of the Father and of the Son and of the Holy Spirit, and teaching them to obey everything that I have commanded you." And then he promised, "And remember, I am with you always, to the end of the age" (Matthew 28:19-20).

In the Book of Acts, Luke tells the story slightly differently, saying that Jesus instructed the disciples to wait in Jerusalem for the Holy Spirit: "You will receive power when the Holy Spirit has come upon you; and you will be my witnesses in Jerusalem, in all Judea and Samaria, and to the ends of the earth" (Acts 1:8). With different words, both Matthew and Luke record the mission Jesus gave his disciples, a misson we call the Great Commission. They were to devote the rest of their lives to being his witnesses and continuing the work he had begun.

It's clear as we read the rest of Acts 1 that Jesus' followers did not simply pray; they also prepared for their work in taking Jesus' message to the world. Within a week, while they were praying together, the Holy Spirit fell upon them and they launched the church, preaching the gospel, inviting people to faith, baptizing, teaching, meeting together in homes, worshiping in the Temple courts, and sharing with any who had need. Where would Mary have been? I believe she saw Christ's commission as her continuing mission and that she devoted the rest of her life to this mission that God had given her.

Jesus had told his disciples to be light to the world. He had told his followers to teach others what he had taught them. He had told them to be his witnesses. Don't you imagine this is what Mary did during the last days of her life? I believe she would have continued to do the things Jesus had done—to look for people who were lost sheep and bring them back to God; to find those who were hungry and thirsty and sick and naked and in prison and care for them; to let her light so shine before others that they might see her good works and give glory to her Father in heaven; to love her neighbor and love her enemy and do the things Jesus had called all the disciples to do. Wouldn't Mary have devoted the next fifteen years of her life to doing those things?

That takes me back to where we began—on Long Island, New York, at a Walmart at 4:55 a.m. on Black Friday. It was cold. People had been in line for hours. They each had that one, two, or three things they most wanted to buy—a gift for a parent, a child, a friend, or even themselves. Someone started to open the doors and then closed them. The crowd surged forward. The doors gave way. The crowd rushed in. A store employee went down. There were, however, a handful of people who stopped and tried to help the employee. They tried to create a human barricade around Jdimytai Damour. But most of the people just hurried by, intent on getting the bargains they had stood in line for.

> Our mission at Christmas is not to get stuff for
> people to open on Christmas morning.
> It is to be people of hope who let
> Jesus' light shine through them.

There were two thousand people in front of Walmart that morning. How many of them do you think were Christians? Eighty percent? Maybe sixteen hundred people who claimed to follow Jesus Christ. And how many of them stopped to help? Three. Three people. Here's the question I would ask you: Would you have stopped to help?

Our mission at Christmas is not to get stuff for people to open on Christmas morning. It is to be people of hope who let Jesus' light shine through them, who act as his witnesses so that others see him in us, who offer hope and help, who pray and work so that our world looks more like the kingdom Jesus proclaimed. This is what Mary would have been doing. And this is what we are called to do.

This year, how will you offer hope to people who don't have it? How will you offer encouragement and joy? If your Christmas doesn't include serving the poor in some way, you've missed out on part of the mission.

I wonder if Mary celebrated the birthday of Jesus in the years following his ascension. Some have suggested that the ancient Jews did not mark birthdays, and this may be so. But how could Mary not remember and mark the birth of her son each year? And as she did, she would have looked back on Christmas through the lens of Easter, with great hope that one day she would see her son again.

At Christmas we're meant to celebrate the hope of the Resurrection and to remember Christ's Great Commission.

2.

THE PIERCING
OF MARY'S SOUL

The child's father and mother were amazed at what was being said about him. Then Simeon blessed them and said to his mother Mary, "This child is destined for the falling and the rising of many in Israel, and to be a sign that will be opposed so that the inner thoughts of many will be revealed—and a sword will pierce your own soul too." (Luke 2:33-35)

2.

THE PIERCING OF MARY'S SOUL

In the previous chapter we pondered Mary at around sixty years old, facing her own death, and reflecting upon it in the light of the death and resurrection of her son. In this chapter we go back in time, closer to that first Christmas, about fifteen years before Mary's death, to the day when she watched her son die. It was the day we now call Good Friday, but to Mary there was nothing that seemed good about it as she stood at the foot of the cross.

The Day Mary's Soul Was Pierced

The Sanhedrin had arrested Jesus in the middle of the night after he celebrated the Passover Seder with his friends. Jesus had gone to the Garden of Gethsemane to pray. Judas Iscariot, the traitor among his disciples, led the guard there to arrest him. That night he was tried and convicted of blasphemy by the religious leaders. Early the next morning, he was taken by the guard to the Roman governor and charged with leading an insurrection against Rome—a crime punishable by death, usually death by crucifixion.

The Gospels do not tell us where Mary was that night, but we know she was in Jerusalem. If Jesus were your son and you learned he had been arrested, where would you be? I imagine she would have gone to the home of the High Priest that night, arriving after Peter's denial of Christ, to stand in the court-yard. I imagine her watching, weeping, and praying.

Whether or not Mary was at the High Priest's home that night, she would certainly have been present when Jesus was tried before the Roman governor, Pontius Pilate, about six o'clock that morning. Pilate asked the crowd gathered outside his palace, "What would you have me do with this man?" It must have taken Mary's breath away when she heard the crowd shout, "Crucify him! Crucify him!" Pilate asked, "Well, what has he done?" And someone in the crowd answered, "He leads a rebellion against Rome. He claims to be a king, usurping your authority and Caesar's. Crucify him!"

The chief priests knew that accusing Jesus of being a traitor to Rome would ensure that the Romans would make a public example of him. Before sending Jesus to be crucified, Pontius Pilate commanded that the Roman *lictors*, or special attendants, torture him. They stripped him naked. They wrapped a crown of thorns and placed it upon his brow. They beat him with their tools of torture. Then they wrapped a purple robe around his shoulders and mocked him for claiming to be a king. They spit upon him and struck him, all in an effort to dehumanize and break him. They mockingly bowed before him and said, "Hail, king of the Jews." By eight o'clock that morning, they led him back to Pontius Pilate.

Mary would have watched in horror as her son stood there humiliated, a bloody mess. Pontius Pilate presented him to the people, and once more the crowd cried out, "Crucify him! Crucify him!"

Pilate then ordered the guards to take Jesus outside the city walls to a hill called Golgotha where he would be nailed to a cross, hung between two criminals, and left to die a slow and painful death.

Part of the power of Mel Gibson's film *The Passion of the Christ* was in his portrayal of Mary on the day Jesus died. Romanian actress Maia Morgenstern played the part of Mary. She captured well how I imagine Mary on that day, demonstrating strength for her son but showing intense sorrow in her eyes.

Part of what made the film so compelling was seeing the suffering and death of Jesus through the eyes of his mother.

> Though we often picture Jesus on a cross high above the crowds, Romans typically crucified their victims only two or three feet off the ground.

John tells us that Mary stood "near the cross of Jesus" (John 19:25), watching and weeping as they drove spikes into his hands and feet. Finally Jesus' cross was hoisted into the air. He hung there next to two common criminals. Though we often picture Jesus on a cross high above the crowds, Romans typically crucified their victims only two or three feet off the ground. Mary could reach up and touch the chest of her son as he hung on the cross. Their eyes could meet, and Jesus could speak to Mary. Among his final words as he died on the cross was a request of his disciple John to take care of Mary.

Mary stood there for hours, watching helplessly. It would be the longest day of her life. You can imagine the pain she was feeling, the sorrow and the overwhelming grief on this terrible day.

Thoughts of Christmas

What was Mary thinking about during those hours as she waited and prayed for her son to die so his suffering might be ended? I wonder if she might not have cried out to God, *"Why?"* Her son was beautiful, devout, holy, compassionate, just, and kind. How could such a horrible fate befall him? As she tried to make sense of what was happening, I believe she may have remembered Christmas and the things that had happened on the day Jesus was born.

She remembered the magi who had brought Jesus gold, frankincense, and myrrh. Myrrh—what a strange gift to give a child. It was used to make the oil that anointed holy things dedicated to God, and it was used by kings for their scented oils. It was also used, mixed with wine, to deaden the pain of those about to be crucified. In fact, Jesus had just been offered such wine before his crucifixion (Mark 15:23). Myrrh was also used to embalm the dead. Was the magi's gift a sign, she wondered, that God knew her son's fate? Was his painful death somehow part of God's plan?

As she stood there for six hours, did she think about Joseph's words while she was still pregnant? "Mary, I had a dream last night. It was so real. An angel of the Lord appeared to me and said, 'Joseph, son of David, do not be afraid to take Mary as your wife, for the child conceived in her is from the Holy Spirit. She will bear a son, and you are to name him Jesus, for he will save his people from their sins'" (Matthew 1:20-21). Jesus' name in Aramaic, *Yeshua*, means "God saves." Mary and Joseph were obedient and named him Yeshua. How many times over the years had Mary pondered the meaning of that name?

How would he save his people from their sins? What did it mean? Mary may have been the first theologian to ponder how Jesus' death brings about salvation, but she would not be the last.

As Mary stood at the foot of the cross, was she thinking of how the shepherds came running into that cavernous place where she'd given birth among the animals? The shepherds said, "We've come to see the child, for an angel appeared to us and said, 'I am bringing you good news of great joy for all the people: to you is born this day in the city of David a Savior, who is the Messiah, the Lord.' Then a chorus of angels began to sing to us: 'Glory to God in the highest heaven, and on earth peace among those whom he favors'"(Luke 2:10-11, 14). At the time, Mary had pondered these things in her heart. Now surely she remembered the angels' words and wondered, *How can this bloody cross possibly be good news? How could the death of my son bring peace? And what kind of Messiah and Lord submits to crucifixion at the hands of people who are so clearly evil?*

On that terrible day, how could Mary not have been contemplating the words spoken by an old man named Simeon when she took her baby to the Temple for the first time. Simeon held Jesus in his arms, then spoke words that she had often tried to forget: "This child is destined for the falling and the rising of many in Israel, and to be a sign that will be opposed so that the inner thoughts of many will be revealed—and a sword will pierce your own soul too" (Luke 2:34-35). Now, as Jesus hung on the cross, his hands and feet pierced, Mary finally understood what Simeon had meant. Her soul was being pierced by the sword of grief.

Mary must have remembered all these things during that terrible six hours. Why do I believe that? Because the small details surrounding Jesus' birth could only have made their way into our Gospels if Mary had passed them on to others. And if she had passed those details on to others, it would have been years after the death and resurrection of her son. In other words, the details of Christmas Day have come down to us for the same reason Mary would have remembered them at the cross—because they were vitally important.

> We celebrate Christmas with red poinsettias, reminding us of the blood that flowed and the sacrifice that was made that day on Calvary.

Making Sense of the Suffering

For Mary, the hideous cross only made sense in light of the events surrounding Christmas. About thirty-three years before, Simeon had said Mary's soul would be pierced. His words meant that somehow God had known Jesus would be crucified and had had a plan to use Jesus' suffering. It explained Joseph's dream and their son's name meaning "God saves." Did Mary understand all this as she stood at the foot of the cross? I don't believe she did. But did she ponder all these things? How could she not? The key to making sense of her son's suffering and death lay in the words spoken about him before and just after his birth.

We noted that Christmas and Easter are a package deal. So too are Christmas and Calvary—Christmas and the cross. Our family has a Christmas ornament that is the first one we place on the tree every year. It's a spike, about the size and shape of the Roman spikes used to crucify Jesus. It hangs near the trunk of our tree, where most guests who walk into our home will never see it. But we know it's there. We put it on our tree first because it reminds us of why we celebrate Christmas: unto us is born a Savior who is Christ the Lord. It's the same reason we celebrate Christmas with red poinsettias, reminding us of the blood that flowed and the sacrifice that was made that day on Calvary.

Mary was not the only one struggling to make sense of the cross. The disciples would have been struggling too. Jesus had tried to prepare them for this day. On the night before, he had taken bread and given thanks for it, and then blessed it and broke it saying, "This is my body, which is given for you" (Luke 22:19). And he took the cup and he said, "This cup that is poured out for you is the new covenant in my blood" (Luke 22:20). Yet all evidence in the Gospels indicates that the disciples did not understand what was happening on the cross.

What was happening? Here we have a righteous man, an itinerant preacher, teacher, and reformer clashing with the religious authorities—the people who managed to convince the Romans to torture and kill him. It's a tragic story, but there is something more happening here. Jesus didn't die accidentally. He knew in advance what would happen. Luke tells us, "When the days drew near for him to be taken up, he set his face to go to Jerusalem" (Luke 9:51).

Jesus understood that his death would be used by God to save humanity from sin. His life wasn't taken from him. He laid it down. It was the fulfillment of a plan.

It was only after the Crucifixion and Resurrection that the disciples began to make sense of what had happened. They looked at the suffering and death of Jesus, and finally they understood that God was doing something in that moment to save the world. It was Jesus' finest moment. It was an act of salvation for the world, the ultimate act of deliverance. The prophet Isaiah had described this kind of suffering centuries before.

> He was despised and rejected by others;
>   a man of suffering and acquainted
>   with infirmity;
> and as one from whom others hide
> their faces
>   he was despised, and we held him
>   of no account.
> Surely he has borne our infirmities
>   and carried our diseases;

yet we accounted him stricken,
    struck down by God, and afflicted.
But he was wounded for our transgressions,
    crushed for our iniquities;
upon him was the punishment that made
us whole,
    and by his bruises we are healed.

(Isaiah 53:3-5)

Some people believe Isaiah was describing Israel, who in her exile suffered for the sins of the people who had gone before. But Jesus and the apostles understood that Isaiah's words also pointed toward the suffering and death of the Christ.

The Meaning of the Cross

I must admit that *how* Jesus' death brings about our forgiveness remains something of an enigma. This imagery of one person suffering vicariously for another was much clearer to first-century people, who routinely offered animal sacrifices for a variety of reasons. Greeks and Romans sacrificed animals to their gods in order to bribe them for blessings or safety or help. Jews sacrificed animals as offerings of thanksgiving to God, but also to make peace with God—to make amends or to atone for their sin. By bringing an animal as a guilt or sin offering, the sins of the individual were symbolically placed upon the animal. God, by commanding his people to offer these sacrifices, was providing a mechanism for them to confess, to atone for their sin, and to receive forgiveness and grace.

In that first-century world, both Jewish and Gentile followers of Christ could look at the cross and understand that on it God's Son was the gift offered, the sacrifice made. He took upon himself the sins of countless generations of people. He absorbed the sting of sin, the pain of sin, the alienation of sin and rendered it powerless to keep humanity from God.

Imagine here a bee that stings you and then is rendered powerless and finally dies. Jesus takes the sting of sin and death upon himself and renders them powerless.

There, on the cross, a divine drama was played out whose aim was to communicate a message to humanity. The message of any guilt or sin offering is first that sin has been committed and guilt rightly aroused. The cross is thus a pronouncement about human sin. We human beings are broken and are prone to do the wrong thing. As Isaiah said, "All we like sheep have gone astray" (Isaiah 53:6).

But the cross is a pronouncement of more than that. The fact that Christ offered himself as a sacrifice on our behalf tells us that God longs to forgive us, redeem us, and restore us. Christ willingly bears our sins.

> The cross is God's work to set you free and make you right with him. Christ has *already* atoned for your sins.

Some people are prone to feel a great deal of guilt in life. They feel guilty all the time. They were raised to feel guilty. People look at them the wrong way and they feel guilty. But if you're among that group, your struggle with guilt may indicate that you haven't fully understood the cross. The cross is God's work to set you free and make you right with him. Christ has *already* atoned for your sins.

On the other hand, some people seldom feel guilt, even when they should. They don't like to talk about "sin"—it seems too dour a concept. Hence the idea that Jesus would in some way give his life to atone for our sins seems like nonsense. If you're among that group, it may be helpful to look at a standard definition of sin. The word used most often for sin in the New Testament is *hamartia*, which in ancient Greek meant "to miss the mark." The word itself tells us that there is a mark, a right way, and to sin is to miss that ideal or right way. The word sometimes meant a mistake or failure. Among the 173 times the word appears in the New Testament, frequently it pointed to the intentional or instinctive turning away from what is right.[4]

When we look at the world around us, evidence of sin is everywhere. There are dramatic examples, such as the shooting of twenty children and six staff at Sandy Hook Elementary School just before Christmas 2012,[5] the terrible ongoing wars in various parts of the world, or the daily crimes witnessed in our own communities. But we deceive ourselves if we only point to others as the source of evil.

Soviet dissident Alexander Solzhenitsyn's famous quotation is illuminating here: "If only there were evil people somewhere insidiously committing evil deeds, and it were necessary only to separate them from the rest of us and destroy them. But the line dividing good and evil cuts through the heart of every human being. And who is willing to destroy a piece of his own heart?"[6]

I struggle with sin in thought, word, and deed. I have mixed motives that I'm not always self-aware enough to see. At times I am a party to sins committed halfway around the world on my behalf, either through my love for consuming cheap garments and electronics made by workers who may not receive a living wage, or by economic and political policies I don't fully understand and yet support with my votes. And while I strive to live what I preach and believe, I come to the end of each day aware that I have yet to live up perfectly to my ideals.

The cross Mary stood before was a sign, a dramatic act of God in which he was holding a mirror up to humanity as if to say, "There is something dreadfully wrong with you, and you need to be saved." But the message did not end there; in the cross, God was also saying, "I want to save you, and my Son has borne your sin on this cross that you might be set free."

Precisely how Jesus' death saves is a mystery; there are multiple theories of the Atonement, and each carries important truths. Some view the Atonement—God's use of the cross to redeem, forgive, and restore us—as though it were a mathematical, economic, or juridical formula. But to me the cross makes the most sense when I recognize it more as poetry, as a divine drama meant to touch our hearts, move us to repentance, and lead us to acceptance of the truth that we are sinners and Jesus is our Savior. It is meant to lead us to accept a love and mercy that we don't deserve and cannot afford. And it is meant to lead us to an assurance that he has, in the famous words of John Wesley, "taken away my sins, even mine, and saved me from the law of sin and death."[7]

What does Good Friday—Jesus' death on the cross and his atonement—have to do with Advent and Christmas? The child to be born would be the Savior of the World.

As Mary stood by the cross, she listened. There were two common criminals crucified with Jesus, one on each side of his cross. One of them cried out, "Jesus, remember me when you come into your kingdom" (Luke 23:42). Do you remember how Jesus answered? "Today you will be with me in Paradise" (Luke 23:43). Some of the people standing at the foot of the cross continued to hurl insults at Jesus. He prayed, "Father, forgive them; for they do not know what they are doing" (Luke 23:34).

Perhaps it was at this point when Mary fully grasped what was happening on the cross. She must have sensed that Jesus had chosen to suffer when with his last breath he cried out, "It is finished" (John 19:30). As Mary watched and listened during those six hours, helpless and unable to save her son, it's possible she remembered the events of the first Christmas morning and began to understand that, though she could not save him, his suffering would save her and all of humankind.

> Sin alienates us from God, but on the cross God was seeking to help us see the seriousness of our sin, the costliness of our forgiveness, and the magnitude of his love.

In his letter to the Romans, Paul expresses it this way: "We have peace with God through our Lord Jesus Christ. . . . For while we were still weak, at the right time Christ died for the ungodly. . . . God proves his love for us in that while we still were sinners Christ died for us" (Romans 5:1, 6, 8). Sin alienates us from God, but on the cross God was seeking to help us see the seriousness of our sin, the costliness of our forgiveness, and the magnitude of his love.

The baby who was born two thousand years ago was named Jesus—"Savior"—because he would save us from our sins. Only two of the four Gospels record the stories of Jesus' birth and then sparingly. Their focus is on his death, for it was on the cross that God was reconciling the world to himself. The profound gift of Christmas is our salvation and forgiveness. The babe born in Bethlehem would give his life to save us from our sin.

The cross of Christ points us to the brokenness of humankind. But it also demonstrates the magnitude of God's love for us and offers peace with God and salvation through Jesus Christ. The salvation that you and I have received cost Jesus his life. It cost Mary her son.

Our Advent journey, preparing our hearts to celebrate the birth of Jesus Christ, takes us to the cross, where we remember that the Child whose birth we celebrate would be tortured and killed, and that on that cross he gave his life that we might receive life. He bore our sins that we might be free. God is the God of the second chance. And Jesus came to save us from our sins and from ourselves. What wondrous love is this!

Christmas is inextricably linked to Calvary. I once asked one of the men in our church, who had spent time in a federal prison for the possession and sale of drugs, what difference this baby born in Bethlehem had made in his life. The man replied, "Because of Jesus, there is one less drug addict and dealer running amok in Kansas City. I now run amok at our church, helping with our addiction programs and showing inmates at Lansing Prison how they can have a new life in Jesus Christ." He personally knew why Mary had called her child Jesus. When he looked at the cross, he saw his Savior, bearing his sins so that he might be free.

3.

AMAZED, ASTOUNDED, AND ASTONISHED

Now every year his [Jesus'] parents went to Jerusalem for the festival of the Passover. And when he was twelve years old, they went up as usual for the festival. When the festival was ended and they started to return, the boy Jesus stayed behind in Jerusalem, but his parents did not know it. Assuming that he was in the group of travelers, they went a day's journey. Then they started to look for him among their relatives and friends. When they did not find him, they returned to Jerusalem to search for him. After three days they found him in the temple, sitting among the teachers, listening to them and asking them questions. And all who heard him were amazed at his understanding and his answers. When his parents saw him they were astonished; and his mother said to him, "Child, why have you treated us like this? Look, your father and I have been searching for you in great anxiety." He said to them, "Why were you searching for me? Did you not know that I must be in my Father's house?" But they did not understand what he said to them. Then he went down with them and came to Nazareth, and was obedient to them. His mother treasured all these things in her heart. (Luke 2:41-51)

3.

AMAZED, ASTOUNDED, AND ASTONISHED

We visited Mary at her death and, fifteen years earlier, at the cross. Now we journey back further still, and closer to the date of Jesus' birth. Mary is in her twenties. She and her husband Joseph have taken their twelve-year-old son Jesus to Jerusalem for the Passover.

The story of their trip is fascinating for several reasons. One reason is that it's the only story from Jesus' childhood that we have in all the Gospels.

This is it; there are no others. We have the infancy narratives, and then the Gospels skip ahead to Jesus at age thirty, with the exception of this story. (In the second and third centuries, Christians would try to fill in the gaps with all kinds of interesting stories, but the Gospels themselves contain just this one.)

Another reason the story is fascinating is that it's the last time we read about Joseph alive in the Gospels. After this, we no longer hear about him. It's presumed that Joseph died somewhere between the time of this story and the beginning of Jesus' public ministry.

Finally, this story includes the first recorded words of Jesus. Think of it: preserved in the story are the words of Jesus from when he was twelve years old.

So, given that this is the only story in the Gospels about Jesus' childhood, we can't help but ask: Why this story? Why did Mary pass it on to the apostles? And of all the stories she must have told, why did Luke choose this one?

An Astonished Mother

I'll answer the question with a story of my own. When my daughter Rebecca was six, our family took a vacation to Disney World with another family. We were staying at one of the Disney resorts, and the first morning we got ready to leave for the park. We arrived at the tram station early and were shopping in the Disney store. A few minutes later I saw the tram and shouted, "Come on, the tram's here. Let's go!" The tram was so crowded that we couldn't get on it together. The other dad and I got on the front, and my wife LaVon and the other mom and kids got on the back. We were on our way to Disney World!

About a half mile down the road, LaVon called, "Adam, is Rebecca up there with you?" "No," I called back, "I thought she was with you." LaVon screamed, and the brakes slammed on. We shouted for our six-year-old. She was not on the tram. I jumped off and ran like an Olympian back to the store to look for our daughter. There were thousands of strangers all around and I had left my little girl behind!

As I ran, I feared that someone had taken her. Maybe she was in tears, wondering where her parents had gone. When I finally arrived at the gift shop, panting and on the verge of my first heart attack, I found Rebecca shopping away, totally oblivious of the fact that we weren't there. I grabbed her by the shoulders and said, "Becca, what were thinking? Didn't you hear me say, 'Come on, let's go'? Why are you still here? Don't you know what could have happened? Don't you ever do that to me again."

When I was done, I wrapped my arms around her and just held her tight. We got on the tram and went into the park. But I will never forget that experience. And here's the thing—we had been separated for just ten minutes!

> When Jesus was a child, it is estimated
> that more than three hundred thousand people
> poured into Jerusalem for the Passover.

Now let's consider the story from Luke 2. Mary and Joseph had taken Jesus to Jerusalem for the Passover. Every male Jew living within a reasonable distance of Jerusalem was required to be there for the holiday. Many others made long treks to be present. It is estimated that more than three hundred thousand people poured into the city for that week. Mary and Joseph and all their family and friends from Nazareth made the long, arduous journey. It would have taken over a week by caravan.

When Passover ended, Joseph, Mary, and the entire community from Nazareth headed home. After traveling for ten hours, they arrived at their camp. Mary found Joseph and said, "Where's Jesus?" Joseph said, "I thought he was with you." Can you hear Mary shout? They had just lost the Messiah, the Savior of the World, the Son of God!

Joseph and Mary hurried back to Jerusalem. Their sense of panic grew as they searched the city—not just for ten minutes but for three days. They went from house to house. He wasn't there. They went to everyone they knew. He wasn't there. They checked among the sick and injured. He wasn't there. Do you feel what Mary was feeling? Do you understand why, for the rest of her life, she told that story over and over again?

Luke tells us that finally, when Mary and Joseph found Jesus in the Temple, "they were astonished" (Luke 2:48). Now, the word *astonished* doesn't mean they were excited. It means they were dumbfounded. You have got to be kidding. What are you doing here? Why didn't you try to find us?

In that same verse Mary says, "Child, why have you treated us like this? Look, your father and I have been searching for you in great anxiety." Luke uses the Greek word *odunao* to describe how Mary and Joseph felt. *Odunao* is used elsewhere in Luke, in the parable of the rich man and Lazarus, to describe the torments of hell. So when Mary said she and Joseph were in "great anxiety," she was saying they were overwhelmed with sorrow—or perhaps accurately, Jesus had put them through a living hell.

This is a story about parents and children of all generations and ages. This is our story. As parents, we tend to remember and retell those stories. The stories stand out in our minds as pivotal moments. And that is why Mary remembered this episode. It was one of the most traumatic moments in her child-rearing years. She had experienced three days of not knowing what had happened to her son— three days of grief.

Parenting Jesus

Parenting is hard. At times it is filled with great joy, but at other times it can feel like a living hell. We love our children so much and want the best for them.

When my kids were young, I worried about them, and I always thought that when they were older I wouldn't worry so much. Little did I know that as children grow up, you worry *more*. They get their driver's licenses, and they begin to date, and they make friends that you are not so certain about. The harder you push in one direction, the more they push in the opposite direction. They go off to college and you have no idea what they're doing—what harm they might suffer, what decisions they're making that could have lifelong consequences. You don't have control anymore. They start asking questions about their faith and their values, and they wrestle with those things because they're trying to differentiate themselves from their parents. You can't tell them the answers, because they have to find the answers for themselves. Adolescence—what an awful invention.

My girls are remarkable, and I am very proud of them. But you know, it's hard. It's joyful and wonderful and terrifying and awful. My hair turned gray when Danielle became a teenager. My hair began to fall out in clumps when Rebecca became a teenager. I have a bald spot in back, and I think at times it's all her fault. But it's part of the joy and the pain of being a parent. Now I have a granddaughter, and I feel some of that same joy, and anxiety too. If it was hard for Mary and Joseph who were raising the Christ Child, what do you think it's going to be like for you and me who have ordinary children? There comes a point when all that's left to do is pray, keep loving them, and trust them to God.

> We have this image of Christmas and of life that it's supposed to be easy, peaceful, beautiful, and serene. . . . Life does have those moments, but it also has periods of grief and pain and hardship.

We have this image of Christmas and of life that it's supposed to be easy, peaceful, beautiful, and serene. *Silent night, holy night, all is calm, all is bright.*

Life does have those moments, but it also has periods of grief and pain and hardship. Our Scripture reminds us that even Jesus gave his parents fits.

Notice how long Mary and Joseph hunted for Jesus before they found him—three days. Do you remember what else happened after three days? Christ was crucified, and on the third day he was raised. The third day represents the time when darkness turns to light, when our pain or agony or fear is resolved and we can once again feel hope.

A Defining Moment

So, one reason Mary remembered this story was undoubtedly because it was traumatic. But there was a second reason. Often in our lives and our children's lives, the most traumatic moments are also defining moments.

For Mary and Joseph and Jesus, it was a defining moment. I want us to ponder that for a second, because I believe it's one of the reasons Mary told this story and why Luke records it in his Gospel.

When Joseph and Mary finally found Jesus in the Temple, Mary said to him, "Your father and I have been searching for you in great anxiety." And then we hear them, the earliest recorded words of Jesus: "Why were you searching for me? Did you not know that I must be in my Father's house?" (Luke 2:49).

Did you notice that? Mary said, "Your *father* and I have been searching for you." Jesus replied, "I must be in my *Father's* house." Some believe it was there, at age twelve, when Jesus became aware that God was, in a profound sense, his Father in a way that Joseph was not.

For Mary, Jesus' words must have taken her back more that twelve years earlier. She could hear the angel Gabriel speaking to her:

> Do not be afraid, Mary, for you have found favor with God. And now, you will conceive in your womb and bear a son, and you will name him Jesus. He will be great, and will be called the Son of the Most High. (Luke 1:30-32)

There in the Temple, for the first time that we know of, Jesus claimed his special relationship with God, a relationship that would define his life. Some scholars believe that this scene is preserved in the Gospels precisely because it shows Jesus' first affirmation that he was no ordinary boy.

Despite some artistic renderings that show the infant Jesus with an all-knowing expression on his face, Jesus was born into this world a helpless child. He grew and developed. Luke 2:40 notes that he grew in wisdom. Jesus gained understanding over time, until at the age of twelve he became keenly aware: I am God's son and he is my Father in a unique way, unlike anyone else. Now Jesus had to decide whether he was going to trust in that knowledge and accept it.

Interestingly enough, the next time we see Jesus in the Gospels he is thirty years old. John the Baptist is baptizing him, and Jesus hears a voice from heaven saying, "You are my Son, the Beloved" (Luke 3:22).

Throughout the Gospels this relationship of father and son most clearly defined Jesus' relationship with God. He called God his Father. Even at the end of his life, the Sanhedrin convicted him of blasphemy for claiming to be the "Son of God" (Luke 22:70-71).

> No matter what your earthly father was like,
> you have a Father who knit you together in your
> mother's womb, who loves you more
> than you can possibly imagine, who walks
> with you, cares for you, and is relentless in his
> love and mercy and grace toward you.

I want to pause and recognize that some people have had earthly fathers who were abusive or absent or unloving, and thus addressing God as "Father" may not be comforting. Instead it may serve to associate God with a painful figure, one who could not be trusted. For these people, there are many other names and images used in Scripture for God from which they may draw. It is also be possible for these people to allow God to redefine what Father means to them and to see God in a new way that may have profound pastoral implications.

For me, the way I see God as Father has been shaped by my experience as a father to my two girls. As they were growing up, every night that I was home I would pray with them at bedtime. Often after they went to sleep I would tiptoe into their bedrooms and whisper in their ears, "Daddy loves you." I loved, and still love, my girls more than I have ever loved anyone in my life. I would, without needing to think about it, lay down my life for them. That's the picture I have of God as our Father. No matter what your earthly father was like, you have a Father who knit you together in your mother's womb (Psalm 139:13), who loves you more than you can possibly imagine, who walks with you, cares for you, and is relentless in his love and mercy and grace toward you. That's part of what I hear when Jesus calls God "my Father" in the Gospels.

Jesus felt an intimate connection and relationship with God. But he also invites us to do the same—to consider God as our Father and parent, and ourselves as God's children. We read in the Gospel of John, "To all who received him, who believed in his name, he gave power to become children of God" (John 1:12).

Many churches confirm children in their faith at the age of twelve because Jesus at that age claimed God as his Father. At confirmation we ask young people to profess publicly their faith and relationship with God, just as Jesus did that day in the Temple. They say to the congregation, in essence, "I choose to trust in God as my creator and heavenly Father, I choose to accept Jesus as my Savior and follow him as my Lord, and I choose to invite the Holy Spirit to dwell in, shape, empower, and guide me." Confirmation is a defining moment in our lives—a time to claim our relationship with God, just as Jesus did in the Temple at age twelve.

Amazed by Jesus

There was a third reason why I think Mary told the story of young Jesus in the Temple and Luke recorded it in his Gospel, and that was the response of the people to Jesus' words. Now bear in mind, he was twelve years old. Picture a twelve-year-old you know reading Scripture and then preaching a sermon. Imagine that when he or she is finished preaching, you find your heart deeply moved by the message; the spiritual and theological insight surprises you. That's the response that people had to Jesus that day in the Temple.

After three days of searching, Mary and Joseph found Jesus "in the temple, sitting among the teachers, listening to them and asking them questions. And all who heard him were amazed at his understanding and his answers" (Luke 2:46-47). The word for "amazed" here is the Greek word *existemi*. It doesn't simply mean that people thought,

"He's a smart kid." No, they were "blown away" as they heard him. They were utterly astounded. They were a bit unnerved, because clearly this was no ordinary child. The Greek word *existemi* is used in the New Testament, along with two other Greek words, *ekplesso* and *thambeo*, to denote utter amazement— the kind that leaves you breathless, in awe, and perhaps a bit afraid. The Gospel writers use these three words over and over again. Matthew uses them eleven times, Mark ten times, Luke thirteen times, and John six times—all to describe people's response to Jesus.

Mark uses the word *existemi* again after Jesus calmed the wind and waves: "Then he got into the boat with them and the wind ceased. And they were utterly astounded" (Mark 6:51). We read about people's response to Jesus' miracles: "They were astounded beyond measure" (Mark 7:37) and "the crowds were amazed and said, 'Never has anything like this been seen in Israel'" (Matthew 9:33).

Frequently, as in this episode when he was twelve years old, it was Jesus' words that astonished people. In Matthew's Gospel, the Sermon on the Mount ends with these words: "Now when Jesus had finished saying these things, the crowds were astounded at his teaching, for he taught them as one having authority, and not as their scribes" (Matthew 7:28-29).

Again and again, people responded strongly to Jesus' words. When Jesus spoke to Zacchaeus the week before the Crucifixion, he said, "Zacchaeus, I'll eat with you." And Zacchaeus gave up half of all of his income and returned four times what he had taken unfairly from people (Luke 19:1-10). When Jesus approached James, John, Peter, and Andrew as they fished on the Sea of Galilee, he said to them, "Come and follow me." They heard his words and were astounded, and they decided to leave their nets to follow him (Matthew 4:18-22). Approaching Levi at the booth where he collected taxes, Jesus said to him, "Come and follow me."

Levi immediately closed his tax business to follow him (Luke 5:27-28). That's the kind of impact that Jesus' words had on people.

> Jesus died on the cross for you. That is a great gift of salvation, but it's not all he came to do. Jesus was born to show us the way, teach us the truth, and invite us to find life.

Sadly, some Christians love to celebrate the Christmas story, and then they skip ahead to the Crucifixion and Resurrection. All they seem to know about being a Christian is that "Jesus died on the cross for you and me." Yes, Jesus died on the cross for you and me. That is a great gift of salvation and was a central part of his mission. But it's not all he came to do. Jesus also came—he was born—to show us the way, teach us the truth, and invite us to find life.

Words of Life

Jesus' words astounded and amazed. They had the power to change history, and they still have the power to change our lives. They call us to live for God and to love others. They call us to be light for the world, to love not only our neighbors but our enemies. Jesus asks us to forgive and show mercy even to the person who doesn't deserve our mercy. He beckons us to feed the hungry, clothe the naked, and welcome the stranger. His Sermon on the Mount provides us with an ethic for life. His parables illustrate what life in the kingdom of God is meant to be like.

The earliest followers of Jesus were not called Christians. They were called followers of "the Way." Jesus, by his words and witness, provided the way, the path, the mark. Today, so many of the things we take for granted about how life ought to be were the very things Jesus taught. He called people to take up their crosses, deny themselves, and follow him (Luke 9:23). He taught that to be truly great was to be a servant (John 13:15-16). He called his followers to "do to others as you would have them do to you" (Luke 6:31) and to "love one another" (John 13:34). It's not just that Jesus died to save you from your sins. He lived to show you what it means to be human. He lived to teach you who God is. And he lived to call you to a different way of life.

In the parables about the treasure hidden in a field and the pearl of great price, Jesus said that the kingdom of God is like a gift worth giving up everything else for (Matthew 13:44-46). The kingdom of God was the focus of Jesus' teachings. God reigns and invites us to be part of his kingdom, not just after this life is over, but now. That was Jesus' message. These are words to live by, words to die by. As the old gospel hymn says, they are "wonderful words of life."[8]

This is what we celebrate at Christmas—not only the hope of resurrection and the gift of salvation, but the map that helps the lost find their way, the light that helps illuminate our darkness, the truth that's worth giving up everything to have. The Gospel of John tells the story this way:

> In the beginning was the Word, and the Word was with God, and the Word was God. . . . In him was life, and the life was the light of all people. . . . And the Word became flesh and lived among us, and we have seen his glory, the glory as of a father's only son, full of grace and truth. (John 1:1, 4, 14)

Jesus was the Incarnation of God's message and God's will. The messenger was the message.

Jesus was the Incarnation of God's message and God's will. The messenger was the message. When we talk about Jesus as *Savior*, we're referring to the cross and the Resurrection. When we talk about Jesus as *Lord*, we're referring to his call to follow him and to do as he commanded. Do you remember Jesus' last words before he ascended to heaven?

> Go therefore and make disciples of all
> nations, baptizing them in the name of the
> Father and of the Son and of the Holy Spirit,
> and teaching them to obey everything that I
> have commanded you. (Matthew 28:19-20)

At Christmas we're not only celebrating the hope of resurrection and the gift of salvation and the cross, we're celebrating the birth of the One who came to teach us how to live, to show us the way, to be the truth and the life. Because we are his followers, we seek to live our lives in a radically different way. The words of Jesus, Mary's twelve-year-old son, amazed those who first heard him in the Temple. His words amaze and astound us still.

4.

MARY, FULL OF GRACE

In the sixth month the angel Gabriel was sent by God to a town in Galilee called Nazareth, to a virgin engaged to a man whose name was Joseph, of the house of David. The virgin's name was Mary. And he came to her and said, "Greetings, favored one! The Lord is with you." But she was much perplexed by his words and pondered what sort of greeting this might be. The angel said to her, "Do not be afraid, Mary, for you have found favor with God. And now, you will conceive in your womb and bear a son, and you will name him Jesus. He will be great, and will be called the Son of the Most High, and the Lord God will give to him the throne of his ancestor David. He will reign over the house of Jacob forever, and of his kingdom there will be no end." (Luke 1:26-33)

4.

MARY,
FULL OF GRACE

In this chapter we travel further back in Mary's life. Mary is thirteen or fourteen years old, and she's living in her hometown, the tiny village of Nazareth. Nazareth was so insignificant that it didn't even show up on first-century maps. In that village, Mary was on the lowest rung of Jewish society. She was a peasant girl, not a citizen of Rome, not of any importance in and among her own people. It was to this girl that the angel Gabriel appeared, announcing that she would give birth to the long-awaited messianic king.

We call this event the Annunciation. It's a great story, not only for what it tells us about Mary, but for what it teaches us about God and God's ways.

Why Mary?

The story begins with God's messenger, Gabriel, appearing in this small village in a remote part of the Roman Empire. Gabriel, whose name means "hero of God," appeared as a mere man—no wings are mentioned—just an unusual man who showed up on Mary's doorstep one day. He had come looking specifically for this girl, for she was about to play a monumental role in human history. She would give birth to the long-awaited messianic King. Today, more than two thousand years later, one third of the world's population still honors him as their King. God chose Mary for the task of bringing this child into the world.

> There was no one who ever had a greater
> connection to Jesus Christ, no one who
> ever experienced and was a more
> central part of God's plan than Mary.

But why Mary? The early church spoke of Mary as *Theotokos*—a Greek title meaning "God bearer" or one who gives birth to God. She bore God the Son in her womb. No one was ever closer to God. There was no one who ever had a greater connection to Jesus Christ, no one who ever experienced and was a more central part of God's plan than Mary. Why this girl? Why did God send the angel Gabriel to Nazareth to find her?

Gabriel didn't explain God's choice, but Mary interpreted God's actions for us in the words of praise that she sang shortly after discovering she was pregnant. It happened when Mary went to stay with her older cousin Elizabeth for the first three months of her pregnancy. Immediately upon seeing her, Elizabeth felt her own baby, who would become known as John the Baptist, leap in her womb. Elizabeth said to Mary, "Blessed are you among women" (Luke 1:42). Upon hearing Elizabeth's words, Mary broke out in song, inspired by Hannah's song when she gave birth to Samuel hundreds of years before (1 Samuel 2:1-10.)

And Mary said,

> "My soul magnifies the Lord,
>   and my spirit rejoices in God
>   my Savior,
> for he has looked with favor on the
>   lowliness of his servant. . . .
> He has shown strength with his arm;
>   he has scattered the proud in the
>   thoughts of their hearts.
> He has brought down the powerful
> from their thrones,
>   and lifted up the lowly;
> he has filled the hungry with
> good things,
>   and sent the rich away empty."
>   (Luke 1:46-48, 51-53)

Why did God choose Mary? Because God looks with favor on the lowly. He lifts them up, blessing the hungry while scattering the proud, bringing down the powerful and sending the rich away empty. Mary believed that God chose her precisely because she was not of noble birth. Her qualifications were that she was humble, she had a heart for God, and she would be willing to offer herself wholly to God.

This idea of who receives God's favor is a consistent theme in Scripture. God chooses the humble, the unlikely, and the lowly. God chose the elderly Abraham and Sarah to bring forth the chosen people. He chose Moses, a fugitive from the law, a man who stuttered and was tending sheep, to be the lawgiver and deliverer of Israel. He chose David, the shepherd boy, the youngest and scrawniest son of Jesse, to be Israel's greatest king. And he chose Mary, a peasant girl in Nazareth, to bear the Messiah.

Mary no doubt taught Jesus about God's preference for the humble. It's an important theme in Jesus' ministry, and we hear it in his words again and again: "For all who exalt themselves will be humbled, and those who humble themselves will be exalted" (Luke 14:11). "Whoever wishes to become great among you must be your servant" (Mark 10:43). "The last will be first, and the first will be last" (Matthew 20:16).

When Jesus chose disciples, he didn't select the seminary-trained or those with doctorates in theology. No, he chose fishermen, tax collectors, and other unlikely candidates. He taught them humility by washing their feet at the Last Supper and then told them, "I have set you an example, that you also should do as I have done to you" (John 13:15). Jesus told his disciples, "The Son of Man came not to be served but to serve, and to give his life as a ransom for many" (Mark 10:45). This theme of humility is seen throughout the New Testament.

The entire Christmas story is, in part, a story about the reversal of values in God's kingdom. Mary, a peasant girl, was chosen to bear the King. Jesus was born in a stable because there was no room in the inn. The first people God invites to see the Christ are the night-shift shepherds. The story is a call for us to humble ourselves before God.

> Pride is a dangerous sin. It eats away at our soul. It convinces us that we are better than others, we deserve more, and we are above the law.

Pride is a dangerous sin. It eats away at our soul. It convinces us that we are better than others, we deserve more, and we are above the law. It convinces political leaders and CEOs that they can do as they wish without repercussion. But these people are eventually humbled.

The author of First Peter wrote about pride, "'God opposes the proud, but gives grace to the humble.' Humble yourselves, therefore under the mighty hand of God, so that he may exalt you in due time" (1 Peter 5:5-6). God opposes the proud. They eventually fall.

What does this mean for people who are successful? If the rich are sent away hungry and the poor are lifted up, what does it mean for people who are not hungry or poor? It means that we ought to humble ourselves before God. As the Apostle Paul wrote in Philippians:

> Do nothing from selfish ambition or conceit, but in humility regard others as better than yourselves. Let each of you look not to your own interests, but to the interests of others. Let the same mind be in you that was in Christ Jesus. . . . He humbled himself and became obedient to the point of death. (Philippians 2:3-5, 8)

This is a call to humility.

It's easy for pride to sneak into our lives, especially when we're in places of privilege. For some of us, that privilege is based on race; for some it's socioeconomic status; for some it's the fact that we live in the United States and not somewhere else. We begin to think the world revolves around us and to treat others as though they're beneath us. It can happen at the shopping mall when the cashier is a little flustered and can't quite get it right, and finally you get your turn and treat the cashier poorly. Why? Because you can—because you're the customer and that person is the employee or the waitperson at the restaurant or your spouse or your parent or your child or your neighbor.

The passage from First Peter reminds us that God opposes the proud. One of the things I've noticed is that you're going to be humbled one way or another. You either humble yourself, or God will do it for you. When God does it for you, maybe you show up on the front page of the newspaper, or your family and everyone in the neighborhood knows about it, and you're humiliated and brought low. How much better it is to humble yourself before God—to say, "God, please help me remember who I am and that my life is a gift and that anything good ultimately comes from you. Help me to live like that and to treat people well."

God chose Mary, a young girl from an insignificant part of the Roman Empire, to give birth to Jesus because that's how God works. God opposes the proud and gives grace to the humble.

Full of Grace

When Gabriel came to Mary, he said, "Greetings, favored one! The Lord is with you" (Luke 1:28). Some of you may know this passage as the Hail Mary or Ave Maria prayer: "Hail Mary, full of grace, the Lord is with you." The words "favored one" and "full of grace" are a translation of one word in Greek; the word is *kecharitomene*.

At the root of the word *kecharitomene* is the Greek word *charis*. This word is also found in the passage from First Peter: "God opposes the proud, but gives grace [*charis*] to the humble" (1 Peter 5:5). This word appears 170 times in the New Testament in one form or another. Eighty-seven of those times, *charis* is translated as "grace."[9]

So, Mary is full of grace. What does that word mean? It's one of those words we freely throw around, and after awhile it begins to lose its meaning. We sing about "Amazing Grace." We say grace at mealtimes. Someone who is beautiful and acts in a certain way is said to be stylish or graceful. What does the word *grace* mean in the New Testament?

Paul begins most of his letters with the words "Grace and peace to you," and he ends them with the words "May the grace of our Lord Jesus Christ be with you." In the New Testament we read that we stand in God's grace (1 Peter 5:12), live in God's grace (Acts 13:43), and are saved by God's grace (Ephesians 2:5). We approach God in times of need asking for his grace (Hebrews 4:16). In the New Testament, the meaning of "grace" changes depending on context.

Grace is God's kindness, his love, his care, his work on our behalf, his blessings, his gifts, his goodness, his forgiveness, and his salvation. But it is more than that—it is all these things when they are undeserved, when they are pure gift. Further, grace has the power to change our lives.

Grace is at the center of what God was doing in Christmas. God was gracious to Mary. She was "full of grace" because God had chosen her even though she didn't deserve it. Yet God said, "I want to give to you; I want to bless you. I want to give you the honor of bearing the Christ Child." In the biblical account of Christmas we have this wonderful picture of God's graciousness. Mary, full of grace, will give life to the One who is the very embodiment of grace.

The child to be born of Mary was grace incarnate. His life would be a message of grace. He would demonstrate grace to sinners, tax collectors, and prostitutes. These people had been taught that they had no place in the synagogue and that God's judgment and wrath was upon them. Jesus devoted his life to showing them—and us—that God's love, mercy, and kindness are offered to us all. He showed us grace.

> Grace changes the one who receives it,
> and it also changes the one who gives it.

Grace has power. When you give kindness, compassion, goodness, and love to someone who does not deserve it, that graceful act has the power to change hearts, heal broken relationships, and reconcile people and even nations. Grace changes the one who receives it, and it also changes the one who gives it. Think about the period after World War II when allied troops were in Germany and Japan. These were our former enemies, yet we worked side by side with them to rebuild their countries. Grace transformed our enemies into our friends. That's how it's supposed to work.

Grace can transform our own lives too. We find other people changed when we're kind to them even though they might not deserve it. We also find our own hearts changed by that process.

Fred Claus, a movie that came out a few years ago, is the story of Santa's long-lost brother. Fred is in trouble and needs financial help, so he calls his brother Nick at the North Pole. Nick says, "Well, I'll give you the help you need if you'll come and work with me this Christmas." Fred, who is desperate, agrees. Santa puts him to work at a specific task: determining whether children have been naughty or nice.

We're familiar with the routine, right? The naughty children don't receive gifts, and the nice kids do. But an interesting thing happens to Fred as he does this task. Looking at the kids who have been labeled naughty, he begins to see things differently. The kids are not naughty. Sure, they do naughty things, but there's something special about every one of them. What's more, often the reason they do naughty things is because they were hurt or wounded or misled or misguided. Fred comes to believe that the kids most in need of a gift are the naughty ones. Maybe that gift—receiving kindness when they don't deserve it—would change them.

And what do we call that? Grace.

When Jesus ministered with the people of his day, did he go to the nice kids or the naughty kids? In Luke 7, we read that Jesus was eating supper with one of the "nice kids," a Pharisee named Simon. As they ate, someone knocked on the door, and Simon was aghast to see that it was the town prostitute. The woman wept at Jesus' feet and wiped his feet with her hair. Why did she do it? Because she had received grace from Jesus. He, unlike any other religious figure she'd ever met, demonstrated love, kindness, compassion, and forgiveness. Grace changed her. Simon, meanwhile, could do nothing but look with scorn on this woman. When we don't have grace, do you know what fills the gap? It's pride. God opposes the proud. He gives grace to the humble.

Jesus was the incarnation of grace, the embodiment of it. He came to bring us grace and show us what God is like. When he sought out tax collectors and prostitutes, when he told stories of the prodigal son and other sinners, he was demonstrating God's kindness toward all, in the hope that seeing grace in action might change us. When Jesus hung on the cross, giving us a gift that we don't deserve, he wanted to change our hearts so that we would follow him in grace.

The Apostle Paul grew up believing that if he were good enough, God would love him. If he could just obey all the laws, God would show kindness to him. But in his mind, there was always the question of whether he had achieved those goals and was deserving. Then Jesus came, offering the love and mercy of God to all. It turned Paul's world upside down. His theology was blown apart when he came into contact with the gospel of Jesus Christ, because he realized that God already loved him and had reached out to him. God accepted him and wanted him. Paul described this gospel in Ephesians: "For by grace you have been saved through faith, and this is not your own doing; it is the gift of God—

not the result of works, so that no one may boast"
(Ephesians 2:8-9).

That brings us back to Gabriel's words when he
spoke with Mary. He told Mary she would have a
child. Through him, God was blessing this humble
girl with the most remarkable gift and call. She would
literally be filled with grace, as the child forming in
her womb was the embodiment of grace.

> And the Word became flesh and lived among
> us, and we have seen his glory, the glory as
> of a father's only son, full of grace and truth.
> . . . From his fullness we have all received,
> grace upon grace. The law indeed was giv-
> en through Moses; grace and truth came
> through Jesus Christ. (John 1:14, 16-17)

Christmas is about God's grace—the kindness,
love, forgiveness, and blessings being given to us
though we do not deserve them.

Christmas is about God's grace—the kindness, love, forgiveness, and blessings being given to us though we do not deserve them. Jesus came to show God's grace to humankind. And so, during the season of Christmas, as we celebrate the hope of resurrection, the gift of salvation and the cross, and the coming of the One who taught us how to live, we celebrate the gift of grace.

As you ponder the richness of grace during this Advent season, remember that when you receive grace, you're meant to give it away. Christmas is a wonderful time of year to share grace. Is there someone you know who has wronged you or hurt you, someone who does not deserve your kindness or a gift or even a Christmas card? What would happen if you showed this person grace? It might transform him or her, and surely it would transform you.

Favored . . . and Afraid

The angel Gabriel announced that Mary was highly favored and full of grace. She was blessed among all women. You would think that if you were blessed by God in this way, things would be easier. Instead they got harder, and they ended on a cross.

My oldest daughter, Danielle, recently gave birth to our first grandchild. Danielle suffered terrible morning sickness during the first four months of her pregnancy, getting sick multiple times each day. She gave birth in the midst of her second year of law school, so her pregnancy came at a most inconvenient time. And yet in spite of all that, it was a wonderful blessing that has changed our lives.

For Mary, the Annunciation brought with it adversity, hardship, and fear. But it also brought the greatest joy she could ever imagine, and to this day she continues to be honored for her role in God's saving plans.

There are many things to be learned from Mary's experience. I invite you this Advent to ponder them as Mary did: God chooses and uses the humble, so if we humble ourselves before God, he will lift us up.

The gift of Christmas is in part the gift of grace—grace incarnate in Jesus, embodying God's offer of love, mercy, and life to sinners who don't deserve it. Once grace is received, we're meant to extend it to others, which is why Christmas is a wonderful time to give others what they may not deserve—kindness and mercy and love—in the hope that they, along with each of us, might be saved.

Above all, remember during this special season that the blessed, God-favored, grace-filled life is sometimes difficult and challenging. It was not a silent night for Mary, and it may not be for us. But through it all, in the midst of adversity, God is at work. Trust in God.

5.

IT WAS NOT A SILENT NIGHT

In those days a decree went out from Emperor Augustus that all the world should be registered. This was the first registration and was taken while Quirinius was governor of Syria. All went to their own towns to be registered. Joseph also went from the town of Nazareth in Galilee to Judea, to the city of David called Bethlehem, because he was descended from the house and family of David. He went to be registered with Mary, to whom he was engaged and who was expecting a child. While they were there, the time came for her to deliver her child. And she gave birth to her firstborn son and wrapped him in bands of cloth, and laid him in a manger, because there was no place for them in the inn. (Luke 2:1-7)

5.

IT WAS NOT A SILENT NIGHT

In 1816, an Austrian priest named Josef Mohr wrote the words to a Christmas carol for his own congregation, to be sung on Christmas Eve. The carol became so popular that it was translated into virtually every language, and to this day it is probably the best known and loved of all Christmas carols. Even if you seldom go to church, you probably know its words by heart:

Silent night, holy night,
all is calm, all is bright
round yon virgin mother and child.
Holy infant, so tender and mild,
sleep in heavenly peace,
sleep in heavenly peace.[10]

These words have shaped the way we imagine that first Christmas. It was idyllic. It was lovely. It was wonderful. It was joyous. It was perfect. Other Christmas carols capture much the same idea. In "Away in a Manger" we sing, "The cattle are lowing, the baby awakes, but little Lord Jesus, no crying he makes."[11]

The challenge for us is that our own Christmases seldom measure up to this ideal. They're not perfect. They're messy. They're challenging. They're difficult. In our world there's adversity. There's darkness. There's pain and suffering. So on one hand we have the perfect Christmas with Mary and Joseph and the baby. And then there's our Christmas, and it's far from perfect. During this season, many of us struggle with that disparity.

A study conducted a few years ago by the National Women's Health Resource Center found that two-thirds of all women reported feeling depression during the holidays.[12] I suspect that the number of men depressed isn't far behind that. Our Christmas isn't much like the first Christmas.

Or is it?

Not Silent in Bethlehem

Several years ago, Andrew Peterson wrote a wonderful song describing the first Christmas, called "Labor of Love."[13] It described the difficulty of that first Christmas and noted in its opening line, "It was not a silent night." For Mary, that first Christmas was fraught with pain and disappointment.

Luke tells us that Caesar Augustus, emperor of Rome, decreed that a census be taken and that everyone return to the ancestral village of the head of the household. Mary and Joseph were living in Nazareth, but Joseph's ancestral village, his hometown, was Bethlehem. The Roman authorities did not care that Mary was nine months pregnant. She and Joseph were forced to make the eighty- to ninety-mile journey from Nazareth to Bethlehem, which might have taken nine or ten days for a pregnant woman on foot. (Modern-day illustrations often show Mary riding on a donkey, but the Scriptures are silent on that point.) I walked portions of this journey several years ago. The first few days the terrain is flat. After that it's uphill, traversing mountains and valleys for days. It's likely that on the trip, tears were shed. If Mary was like any other expectant mother, she would have felt anxious and probably fearful. And then there were the questions that must have been running through her mind: Where will we stay? Who will help with the birth? Will my child survive?

There was little to mitigate the pain of childbirth in Mary's day except for the comfort of her mother, close friends, and a good midwife.

Mary had been planning to have her child in her home, likely in a room that may have been added to her parents' home in Nazareth. There was little to mitigate the pain of childbirth in that day except for the comfort of her mother, close friends, and a good midwife. It's not hard to imagine Mary's disappointment in being forced to travel to Bethlehem to have her child without any of those.

The disappointment got worse when they arrived in Bethlehem. First-century birthing practices in the best of circumstances were quite different from what we experience today. Here is a description of a modern birthing room from one hospital website:

> Each room feels far more like a resort spa than a hospital. Relax in the whirlpool tub. Stretch out in a queen-size bed (for your partner to share, if you wish). Admire your newborn sleeping nearby in the in-room crib. Enjoy the attention of nurses who pamper the entire family. Pop your favorite CD in our entertainment center.[14]

Now let's look at Luke's description of Mary's birthing room:

> The time came for her to deliver her child. And she gave birth to her firstborn son and wrapped him in bands of cloth, and laid him in a manger, because there was no place for them in the inn. (Luke 2:6-7)

Luke doesn't actually tell us that Mary was in a barn with sheep and goats, with the cattle "lowing." He does tell us there was a manger, which was a feeding trough for animals. Where would this feeding trough have been? Early church tradition has it located in a stable or cave behind or under a house. (The word for that location, often referred to as "inn" in the Bible, is better translated as "guest room.") In those days, people often brought their sheep in at the end of the day and kept their donkeys overnight to be tended. In other words, think of the place where Mary gave birth as a first-century parking garage. It was a far cry from CD players and queen-sized beds.

As to a "silent night," the Scriptures don't mention it. After all, on that first Christmas Mary *gave birth*! I don't imagine it was silent. It would have been filled with noise, not just the sound of the donkeys but the clamor and cries surrounding childbirth.

Keep in mind that Mary was blessed by God, chosen as his handmaiden, and given the most important task any human being would ever have. Her child was the King of kings. She would be the mother of Jesus Christ. She was in the midst of the most profound thing God would do in the history of humankind. And Mary had to bring forth this child among animals, in a place she didn't want to be. God does not promise that life will be easy, that all will be calm and bright. God promises that in the midst of the animal dung and the noise and the disappointment, he is at work!

Think about it: if all were calm and bright in the world, Christmas wouldn't be necessary. Christmas came because the world is broken. We wrestle with sin and are plagued by tragedy. We are confused about what really matters and how we're meant to live.

When referring to our sin, brokenness, hopelessness, and despair, the Bible often describes it in terms of darkness. Matthew quotes Isaiah 9:2: "The people who sat in darkness have seen a great light, and for those who sat in the region and shadow of death light has dawned" (Matthew 4:16). John writes in his Gospel, "In him was life, and the life was the light of all people. The light shines in the darkness, and the darkness did not overcome it" (John 1:4-5).

> This idea that Christ brings light to the world was the inspiration for the date chosen by Christians to celebrate Christmas.

This idea that Christ brings light to the world was the inspiration for the date chosen by Christians to celebrate Christmas. No one knows the day Jesus was born. In ancient times, particularly among the Jews, it appears that birthdays may not have been celebrated. So when Christians contemplated when to celebrate Christ's birth, they chose the winter solstice. Pagans already celebrated the event, which literally is the night when darkness is defeated: after months of the nights growing longer and the days getting shorter, the darkness is turned back; and from that night on, the days grow longer and the nights shorter. The heavens themselves seem to declare the truth of the gospel, "Light shines in the darkness and the darkness did not overcome it."

It was not a silent night for Mary, but she knew that something important was happening. God was working to transform the world. Her baby would change everything.

The Real Gifts of Christmas

I had a friend who once asked me, "When I became a follower of Jesus I expected him to fix the broken things in my life. But I've got as many problems today, maybe more, than when I first became a Christian. What's the point of following him?" I told my friend that we are Christians not because Jesus acts as a magic genie, granting us our daily wishes and delivering us from all adversity; we follow Jesus because we believe that his life, death, resurrection, and teachings offer us the truth about life, strength for the journey, and hope in the face of despair. Following him doesn't change our life situation, but it does change how we look at it and how we live in it.

I follow Jesus, not because I think he's going to make me rich or keep bad things from happening to me. I follow him because I believe that in his life he shows me who God is. In his teachings he shows me how to live. In his death he shows me mercy. And in his resurrection he shows me hope. That's why I follow him.

The Gift of the Way

Jesus once said, "I am the way, and the truth, and the life" (John 14:6). Either this was the most arrogant claim a human being ever made, or it was fundamentally true. Christians believe that it's true. When we listen to Jesus' teachings, they unnerve us and shake us up, and yet we sense they are fundamentally right. We listen to his words and seek to live by them. As we have learned, Jesus' earliest followers, before they were labeled Christians, were called followers of "the Way." The Way was and is a radical departure from the path followed by the rest of the world.

The world calls us to self-indulgence, but Jesus calls us to self-denial. The world calls us to seek our own glory, but Jesus calls us to seek God's glory. The world calls us to pursue a greatness involving accolades and recognition, but Jesus redefines greatness as serving others and calls us to serve without any praise. The world calls us to pursue riches, but Jesus tells us that abundance has nothing to do with possessions. The world calls us to demand justice, but Jesus calls us to demonstrate mercy.

The angels announced to the shepherds, "To you is born this day in the city of David a Savior, who is the Messiah, the Lord" (Luke 2:11). The word *Lord* means master, captain, ruler, and sovereign. Those of us who call Jesus our Lord seek to follow him and do his will rather than our own. In doing so, we find the joy we had been searching for all along. Jesus said, "Those who lose their life for my sake will find it" (Matthew 16:25), meaning that when we follow Jesus and lay aside the life we might have lived, we will find the only life worth living.

> Among the most important gifts God sought to give us at Christmas is the knowledge that we are loved.

The Gift of Love

Among the deepest existential needs of every human being is the need to be loved. We all want to be loved. Among the most important gifts God sought to give us at Christmas is the knowledge that we are loved. John 3:16 is one of the best-known Scriptures in the Bible: "For God so loved the world that he gave his only Son, so that everyone who believes in him may not perish but may have eternal life." Christmas is an expression of God's love for the world.

I learned more about God and theology by being a father than I ever learned in seminary or from a textbook. What I learned is that I love my daughters more than life itself. Sometimes I love them so much it's painful. I long to be in a relationship with them. I love them even when they've hurt my feelings. I want to give them gifts, and I want to bless them. One thing we learn at Christmas is that

God is not a nameless, faceless Higher Power. Jesus came to reveal to us the heart and character of God. He showed us what God is like, through his parables, his life, his witness, and his love for broken people. God knows your name and he loves you, even more than I love my daughters. Others may have rejected you—a coworker, a spouse, your parents, your child. God will never reject you. God's love for you is deeper and wider than you can imagine or believe. Part of the gift of Christmas is unconditional love.

The Gift of Forgiveness and New Life

I have a friend who some years ago got off track in his life. He started making bad decisions. They were little decisions at first, and he thought nobody would find out. But one thing led to another, and things got progressively worse. One day the police showed up at his front door, and he was arrested and ultimately sentenced to jail.

He lost his wife, his dignity, his job. And he lost many of his friends. The one person who refused to reject him was Jesus Christ, who knew everything he had ever done. Jesus spent most of his own ministry with people like my friend. Jesus says to us, "I still believe in what you could be. I will forgive you and will give you a new heart and a new life."

Mary and Joseph each were told that the child born at Christmas was to be named Jesus, which means "God saves." Jesus still saves. At Christmas we celebrate the birth of One who brings mercy, forgiveness, and new life to sinners.

The Gift of the Resurrection

As we learned, Christmas and Easter are inseparable. The One who was born in Bethlehem eventually died and was raised to life. That's the gospel story.

There's a darkness you walk through when you watch a friend or family member die. There's a darkness when you realize that you're mortal and have been given a diagnosis and your days are short. When you're walking through the valley of the shadow of death—through that darkness—where is your light found? The gospel tells us that Jesus Christ died and then, in a way that truly is hard to believe, he rose from the dead.

> Jesus didn't promise that you wouldn't . . . have something tragic happen. What he promised was eternal life. His words don't change your situation; they change your perspective.

Jesus said, "I am the resurrection and the life. Those who believe in me, even though they die, will live, and everyone who lives and believes in me will never die" (John 11:25-26). Notice that Jesus didn't promise that you wouldn't get sick or die in a car accident or have something tragic happen. What he promised was eternal life. His words don't change your situation; they change your perspective.

Christians grieve when we lose our loved ones, but we grieve as those who have hope.

Kathleen Baskin-Ball was just ahead of me in seminary at Southern Methodist University. She and I were youth ministers in the Dallas area and got to know one another through our shared ministry. She stayed in Dallas and went on to serve several churches as a pastor with distinction and as a leader in The United Methodist Church. I came back to Kansas City to start Church of the Resurrection. Kathleen was married and had a little boy. She was loved by her congregations. In January of 2007, Kathleen was diagnosed with a form of cancer that is both aggressive and hard to treat. Kathleen decided to share her journey with her congregation as she sought to fight the cancer.

She continued to preach the gospel every Sunday in her congregation. She didn't just preach it; she lived it. When she could no longer stand up to preach, she continued preaching from a stool.

Then one Sunday she announced to her congregation, "This will be my last sermon as your pastor. I just don't have the strength to do it anymore."

Kathleen knew that some of them had never been baptized, and she offered to baptize any who were ready to become followers of Christ. That Sunday afternoon, thirty-five children and adults came forward to be baptized by her.

That was the last thing Kathleen did as a pastor. A short time later, she went to sleep and awoke in Christ's arms, in that place where Scripture promises that:

> He will wipe every tear from their eyes.
> Death will be no more;
> mourning and crying and pain will be no more,
> for the first things have passed away.
> (Revelation 21:4)

Kathleen lived, proclaimed, and trusted in Jesus, born of Mary, who came to offer us hope and grace and life. That's what we celebrate at Christmas. In the end, light always has the last word.

A Silent Night After All

When we celebrate Christmas, we remember the hope of resurrection—the hope Mary had that she would see her son again. We remember the birth of the One who died on the cross to save us from our sins. We remember that Jesus taught us how to live and love, showing us the way, the truth, and the life.

From the Christmas story we see that those whom God chooses and blesses are not promised that life will be free of adversity, but that in the end the adversity will be worth it because God will work through it. After all, life was not easy for Mary. It most certainly was not a silent night as she gave birth to Jesus, and years later she watched him suffer and die to redeem and save the world.

My wife, LaVon, and I were at the hospital when our daughter Danielle gave birth to our granddaughter.

There were painful contractions, hours of hard labor, doctors and nurses scurrying, and for us, her parents, no small amount of worrying. Then the moment came, and Stella Louise was born. Our son-in-law J. T. came into the waiting room to get us. I will never forget the moment when we saw our daughter, exhausted and yet holding her newborn daughter so tenderly. In that moment, all the pain faded from memory. All the fear and anxiety gave way to love as she held her little girl close.

And that takes me back to Mary. When the shepherds had left, after Joseph had fallen asleep, she put the child to her breast. As she held him near her heart, she found—despite the disappointment, darkness, and pain—a peace, a joy, a love she had never known before. All *was* calm, and all *was* bright.

When we, like Mary, hold Christ near our hearts, we too may discover a silent night after all.

NOTES

1. "Silent Night, Holy Night," Joseph Mohr, 1818; translated by John F. Young, *The United Methodist Hymnal* (Nashville: The United Methodist Publishing House, 1989), 239.

2. Ken Belson and Karen Zraick, "Mourning a Good Friend, and Trying to Make Sense of a Stampede," http://www.nytimes.com/2008/11/30/nyregion/30walmart.html?_r=0.

3. "After the Resurrection," The Catholic Pages, http://www.catholic-pages.com/bvm/resurrection.asp.

4. "Hamartia," http://biblehub.com/greek/266.htm

5. James Barron, "Nation Reels After Gunman Massacres 20 Children at School in Connecticut," http://www.nytimes.com/2012/12/15/nyregion/shooting-reported-at-connecticut-elementary-school.html?pagewanted=all.

6. Aleksandr Solzhenitsyn, *The Gulag Archipelago* (New York: Harper & Row, 1978), 168.

7. "I Felt My Heart Strangely Warmed," Journal of John Wesley, http://www.ccel.org/ccel /wesley/journal.vi.ii.xvi.html.

8. "Wonderful Words of Life," Philip P. Bliss, 1874, *The United Methodist Hymnal* (Nashville: The United Methodist Publishing House, 1989), 600.

9. "Charis," http://biblehub.com/greek/5485.htm.

10. "Silent Night, Holy Night," Joseph Mohr, 1818, *The United Methodist Hymnal*, 239.

11. "Away in a Manger," Ibid., 217.

12. "Most Women Report Holiday Depression," http://www.upi.com/Health_News/2008 /11/28/Most_women_report_holiday _depression/UPI-30341227853095/.

13. The song "Labor of Love" is on the album "Behold the Lamb of God," first released in 2004 by Andrew Peterson, http://www.amazon.com/Behold-Lamb -God-Andrew-Peterson/dp/B0006NNQBQ.

14. "The Birth Place," Olathe Health System, http://www.olathehealth.org/Hospitals-And -Clinics/The-Birth-Place#.U7HrnChlyCY.

ACKNOWLEDGMENTS

I am grateful for a wonderful team of editors and colleagues in ministry at Abingdon Press, including Ron Kidd and Susan Salley, without whom neither this book nor most of my others would ever have been published. I am also grateful to Sally Hoelscher, who worked with my sermon manuscripts to create the first draft of this book.

As always, my deep gratitude goes to the people of The United Methodist Church of the Resurrection for allowing me to be their senior pastor. It is one of the great privileges of my life to serve them

About the Author

ADAM HAMILTON is senior pastor of The United Methodist Church of the Resurrection in Leawood, Kansas, one of the fastest growing, most highly visible churches in the country. *The Church Report* named Hamilton's congregation the most influential mainline church in America and PBS's Religion and Ethics Newsweekly identified him as one of the "Ten People to Watch." In 2013, Adam was invited to deliver the sermon at the National Prayer Service in Washington's National Cathedral as part of the presidential inauguration festivities. A master at explaining questions of faith in a down-to earth fashion, he is the author of many books including *The Journey, The Way, 24 Hours That Changed the World, Enough, Why: Making Sense of God's Will, When Christians Get it Wrong, Seeing Gray in a World of Black and White, Forgiveness, Love to Stay,* and *Making Sense of the Bible.*

SIMON PETER

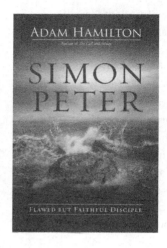

He was not rich or educated, but was familiar with hard work. He was quick-tempered and impetuous, but possessed a passion that would change the world. He left everything to follow his teacher, yet struggled with doubt and fear. Join pastor and author Adam Hamilton in this six-week journey, and take an in-depth dive into the life, faith, and character of Simon Peter. Perfect for Lent or any time of year.

Read *Simon Peter* on your own or, for a more in-depth study, enjoy it with a small group.

ISBN 978-1-5018-4598-7 Hardcover
ISBN 978-1-5018-4600-7 Large print

Also available:
Study resources for children, youth, adults , and a DVD
featuring Adam Hamilton teaching on site in Israel and Italty

THE JOURNEY

Journey with Adam Hamilton as he travels from Nazareth to Bethlehem in this fascinating look at the birth of Jesus Christ. As he did with Jesus' crucifixion in *24 Hours That Changed the World*, Hamilton once again approaches a world-changing event with thoughtfulness. Using historical information, archaeological data, and a personal look at some of the stories surrounding the birth, the most amazing moment in history will become more real and heartfelt as you walk along this road.

Read *The Journey* on your own or, for a more in-depth study, enjoy it with a small group.

ISBN 978-1-5018-2879-9
ISBN 978-1-5018-3604-6 Large Print

CONTINUE THE JOURNEY

Go deeper on your Christmas journey with *A Season of Reflection*. With Scripture, stories, and prayer, this collection of 28 daily readings brings the well-known story into your daily spiritual life.

ISBN 978-1-4267-1426-9

Join Adam Hamilton as he travels the roads to Bethlehem in this video journey. In five video segments, Adam explores Bethlehem, the routes the Holy Family traveled, the traditional site of the stable in Bethlehem, the ruins of Herodium, and more.

ISBN 978-1-4267-1999-8

Study resources for children, youth, and adults and an app for families are also available.
Learn more at JourneyThisChristmas.com

Available wherever fine books are sold.
For more information about Adam Hamilton, visit www.AdamHamilton.org

THE WAY

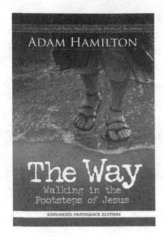

Travel to the Holy Land in this third volume of Adam Hamilton's Bible study trilogy on the life of Jesus. Once again, Hamilton approaches his subject matter with thoughtfulness and wisdom as he did with Jesus' crucifixion in *24 Hours That Changed the World* and with Jesus' birth in *The Journey*. Using historical background, archaeological findings, and stories of the faith, Hamilton retraces the footsteps of Jesus from his baptism to the temptations to the heart of his ministry, including the people he loved, the enemies he made, the parables he taught, and the roads that he traveled.

Read *The Way* on your own or, for a more in-depth study, enjoy it with a small group.

ISBN 978-1-5018-2878-2
ISBN 978-1-5018-3606-0 Large print

Available wherever fine books are sold.
For more information about Adam Hamilton, visit www.AdamHamilton.org

CONTINUE THE WAY

This companion volume to *The Way* functions beautifully on its own or as part of the churchwide experience. Adam Hamilton offers daily devotions that enable us to pause, meditate, and emerge changed forever. Ideal for use during Lent, the reflections include Scripture, stories from Hamilton's own ministry, and prayers.

ISBN 978-1-4267-5252-0

Join Adam Hamilton in the Holy Land as he retraces the life and ministry of Jesus Christ in this DVD study. Perfect for adult and youth classes, the DVD includes a Leader Guide to facilitate small group discussion about the book, the devotions, and the DVD. Each session averages ten minutes.

ISBN 978-1-4267-5253-7

Study resources for children, youth, and adults are also available.

Available wherever fine books are sold.

For more information about Adam Hamilton, visit www.AdamHamilton.org

Made in United States
Orlando, FL
07 November 2023

38676174R00085